I'm Going to See Mr. Hope

Written by Sherry Johnson

Illustrations by Nicholas Howard

I'm Going to See Mr. Hope

WRITTEN BY SHERRY JOHNSON

ILLUSTRATIONS BY NICHOLAS HOWARD

For Ages 3 and Up

For information regarding permissions,
email Sherry Johnson @ sherrybj3@gmail.com

ISBN# 978-1-66640-919-2

Illustrated by Nicholas Howard

Mr. Christopher Coleman for
I Think For You Consulting.

Published by NuVision Publishing
www.nuvisiondesigns.biz

Acknowledgements:

To my wonderful husband, Craig, and three children; Ashley, Chasity and Joshua, thank you for being my biggest cheerleaders and inspiration for this book. Your unwavering support and encouragement made me believe that I can do anything.

I dedicate this book to every child and child-at-heart. This book was written with you in mind. Enjoy!

I'm Going to See Mr. Hope

Little Miss Chaseley woke up early one morning on a mission. She said, "I'm going to see Mr. Hope." So, she jumped out of bed and put on her favorite purple rain boots.

Chaseley walked up to her mom and said, "Mommy, I need to go see Mr. Hope." Her mom said, "Okay, Chaseley. Let me get my keys."

Mommy, Daddy and Chaseley hopped in the car. Mommy buckled Chaseley in her car seat and then Mommy and Daddy buckled up and went on their way.

On the way to see Mr. Hope, Chaseley saw the family's baker. Chaseley said, "He looks very sad, Mommy. May we ask Mr. Baker if he wants to go with us to see Mr. Hope?" Her mom asked Mr. Baker, and he said, "I sure do. I'm feeling really sad."

SCHOOL!

As Mommy, Daddy, Chaseley and Mr. Baker traveled to
see Mr. Hope, Chaseley wanted to stop by the school to
see Mrs. Teacher. Mrs. Teacher looked really worried.
Chaseley understood that look because her Mommy has
had the same look before. Chaseley said, "Mommy, may
we ask Mrs. Teacher if she would like to go with us to see
Mr. Hope?" Her Mom asked, and Mrs. Teacher said,
"I sure do! I am really worried about some things."

STO
OPEN

Mrs. Teacher hops in the car with Mommy and Daddy, Chaseley and Mr. Baker to go see Mr. Hope. While traveling, Mrs. Teacher asked, "Chaseley, where does Mr. Hope live?" Chaseley answered with a slight giggle, "Oh, Mr. Hope lives in different places."

Mommy, Daddy, Chaseley, Mr. Baker and Mrs. Teacher finally arrive at Mr. Hope's special place. Everyone stood outside and waited. Mr. Hope walked out of the house and up to the gates. Chaseley said with a loud voice and big smile, "Hi, Mr. Hope! I brought some friends to see you today!" Mr. Hope replied, "Hi, friends!"

Mr. Hope said, "So, tell me, friends,
why did you all come today?"
"I'm sad," said Mr. Baker.
"I'm worried," said Mrs. Teacher.
Chaseley asked Mr. Hope, "Can you help us?"
Mr. Hope smiles and says, "I sure can."

Everyone left Mr. Hope's special place with a BIG SMILE.
They were no longer sad or worried.
(So, what did Mr. Hope do to help Chaseley and her friends?)

Mommy, Daddy and Chaseley arrived home safely after taking Mr. Baker and Mrs. Teacher home. As Chaseley removed her favorite purple boots, her Mommy smiled and asked, "Miss Chaseley, did you get what you needed from Mr. Hope?" Chaseley answered, "Yes, ma'am, I sure did!"

I just did what Mr. Baker and Mrs. Teacher did.
Her Mom asked, "What was that, Chaseley?" With a
big smile, Chaseley replied, "I listened to HOPE,
not my sadness—not my fear!"

Coloring Pages

The fun isn't over!

Explore your inner artist by adding your favorite colors to Little Miss Chaseley and her favorite boots.

1

WHAT DOES HOPE LOOK LIKE TO YOU? FIRST, COLOR THE TITLE. NEXT, DRAW WHO OR WHAT INSPIRES YOU BELOW THE TITLE.

I'm Going to See Mr. Hope

2

DRAW WHAT HOPE LOOKS LIKE TO YOU BELOW.